AN EXEGETICAL STUDY OF MARK 7:19

DID JESUS ABROGATE THE DIETARY LAWS IN THE TORAH?

Pr. Ebenezer Ankomah
LOVE, OBEY AND LIVE MINISTRY
SEPTEMBER, 2020

DEDICATION

This book is dedicated to the almighty God, my lovely wife and daughter, my immediate family, friends and God's people everywhere who desire to know and obey a "thus saith the Lord." Also to all lecturers and students of the Adventist University of Africa (AUA), Kenya.

TABLE OF CONTENTS

CHAPTER

CHAPTER 1

INTRODUCTION

Mark 7:19 is the most debated verse of the New Testament. In Mark 7:19 we read, "since it enters, not his heart but his stomach, and so passes on? (Thus he declared all foods clean.)." The Greek version reads "ὅτι οὐκ εἰσπορεύεται αὐτοῦ εἰς τὴν καρδίαν ἀλλ᾽ εἰς τὴν κοιλίαν, καὶ εἰς τὸν ἀφεδρῶνα ἐκπορεύεται, καθαρίζων πάντα τὰ βρώματα;"[1] This verse has been used by many modern Christians to substantiate the point that Jesus declared all foods clean, thus abrogating the dietary laws found in the Torah.

---

[1]Unless otherwise stated, all English and Greek Bible references and quotations are from the RSV and Kurt Aland et al. *The Greek New Testament* (Stuttgart: United Bible Society, 2010) respectively.

Problem Statement

Does Mark 7:19 mean Jesus abrogated the dietary laws in the Torah as many scholars have suggested? If so, then there is a big problem. Jesus in Mark 7:9 accused the Pharisees and the scribes of "rejecting the commandment of God." Why would he do the very same thing he accused the Pharisees and the Scribes of doing?

Purpose of the Study

This research seeks to ascertain the true meaning of Mark 7:19 and to establish its connection with the dietary laws in the Torah if any.

Research Objectives

The research seeks to discover how the early recipients of the Gospel according to Mark understood Mark 7:19 and how it is popularly understood among various biblical scholars of our time.

The research again seeks to establish the text in Mark 7:19 since there are variations of the same text in different versions of the Bible. Having this done, the true meaning of the text and its application to modern Christians would be established.

Delimitation of the Study

The main aim of this study is to establish the text in Mark 7:19 and to discover the true meaning of the text. The study will assume that readers already know about the dietary laws in the Torah (Genesis, Exodus, Leviticus, Numbers and Deuteronomy) and so would not spend time on it.

Significance of the Research

This study will help to ascertain the true meaning of Mark 7:19 and its relation to the dietary laws in the Torah. By this, it is hoped to make a meaningful contribution to the food controversy debate among biblical scholars.

Methodology and Procedure

The study adopts a methodology that is in line with its purpose. This is an exegetical paper of Mark 7:19. The study begins with a review of various literature to ascertain the popular view of the text in Mark 7:19. It then proceeds with an exegesis of Mark 7:19 and finally to the theological analysis of the text.

CHAPTER 2

REVIEW OF RELATED LITERATURE

A lot has been written by various biblical scholars on Mark 7:19. The phrase "καθαρίζων πάντα τὰ βρώματα" has been understood differently by various scholars. This section of the paper reviews some of the various literature that deals with the phrase "καθαρίζων πάντα τὰ βρώματα" in Mark 7:19.

Views during the Early Church Period

The early church period spanned from the second to fifth centuries. The contribution of Origen and John Chrysostom on Mark 7:19 is considered in this section.

Origen (185-251 AD)

It is believed that Origen is the oldest Bible commentator who inferred that the phrase "καθαρίζων πάντα τὰ βρώματα" is a Marcan commentary on the previous statement of Jesus. Origen wrote: "When we read in Leviticus and Deuteronomy of the laws about food as clean and unclean …, we are not to think that the scope of the Scripture is found in any superficial understanding of them. For —whatever goes into a person from the outside cannot defile him, since it enters not his heart but his stomach, and so passes on. According to Mark, the Savior —declared all food clean, so we are not defiled when we eat those things declared to be unclean by those who still desire to be in bondage to the letter of the law. But we are then defiled when our lips, which ought to be bound with good judgment as we search for correct balance and weight, speak recklessly and discuss matters we ought not.[2] Thus according to

---

[2]Ancient Christian Commentary on Scripture: New Testament II Mark. Ed. Thomas C. Oden and Christopher A. Hall (Downers Grove, Illinois: InterVarsity, 1998), 124.

Origen, Jesus declared all foods clean in Mark 7:19,
hence abrogating the dietary laws as found in the Torah.

John Chrysostom (354-407 AD)

Chrysostom is among the earliest commentators, after Origen, to adopt the rendering of Mark 7:19 as "this He [Jesus] spoke thus cleansing all meats,"[3] interpreting it to mean that no food makes a man unclean.

Modern Interpretations

Many modern bible scholars have expressed their understanding on Mark 7:19 following the understanding of Origen. Davidson notes that "most of the commentaries since the last century which deal with the issue of food controversy in the NT seem to go in one direction: the NT abolished these laws."[4]

---

[3]Chrysostom *Homilies on Matthew* 51.4 (NPNF, 10:318).

[4]Davidson Razafiarivony, "The New Testament Attitude Toward The Old Testament Distinction Between Clean And Unclean Animals" (Doctor of Philosophy Dissertation, Adventist International Institute of Advanced Studies, Philippines, 2006), 32.

In the Baker exegetical commentary on the NT, it is accepted that the comment "καθαρίζων πάντα τὰ βρώματα; in Mark 7:19 is a Markan interpretive comment that explains an implication of Jesus's teaching in these verses. It is not a comment made by Jesus himself.[5]

According to Marcus, it appeared for Jesus's hearers that he was rejecting the Pharisaic traditions concerning defilement and saying, "a person is not so much defiled by what enters him from outside as by what comes from within."[6]

Again, Witherington, Stettler and Rudolph assert that Mark's comment is an indication that Jesus was passing down a Christological ruling that the arrival of

---

[5]Robert H. Stein, *Baker Exegetical Commentary on the New Testament,* ed. Robert W. Yarbrough and Robert H. Stein, (Grand Rapids: Baker, 2008), 344.

[6]J. Marcus, Mark 1—8: *A New Translation with Introduction and Commentary. Anchor Bible 27.* (New York: Doubleday, 2000), 453.

the kingdom of God had brought the food regulations of the Old Testament to an end.[7]

Taylor also agrees with Marcus that "καθαρίζων πάντα τὰ βρώματα;" is best to be understood as a Markan interpretive comment[8] concerning the implications of Jesus's words in 7:15 and 18b-19.

R. T. France suggests that the present account explained that freedom from the issue of clean versus unclean foods stemmed from Jesus himself. He said that it was not what enters into a person's stomach that defiles one but what comes out of one's heart (7:21). Thus, as Mark points out, he declared all food clean to eat (7:19c). Consequently, the readers' present practice

---

[7]B. Witherington III, *The Gospel of Mark: A Socio-Rhetorical Commentary* (Grand Rapids: Eerdmans, 2001), 228-231. (See also C. Stettler, "Purity of Heart in Jesus' Teachings: Mark 7:14—23 Par. as an Expression of Jesus' Basileia Ethics." Journal of Theological Studies 55 2467—502 and D. J. Rudolph, "Jesus and the Food Laws: A Reassessment of Mark 7:19b." Evangelical Quarterly 74:291-311.)

[8]V. Taylor, *The Gospel according to St. Mark: The Greek Text with Introduction, Notes, and Indexes* (London: MacMillan, 1952), 345.

stems from the teachings of Jesus Christ, the Son of God.[9]

To Bas Iersel, the comment means that "for Jesus' followers the law on clean and unclean foods no longer applies."[10]

Brunt notes that first century Gentile Christians understood Mark 7:19 only as calling all foods clean, including those forbidden in Lev 11.[11]

In the judgment of the Jesus Seminar, Robert W. Funk and Roy W. Hoover and the Jesus Seminar agrees that Mark 7:19c is a Markan comment. But the comment reads differently, "(This is how everything we eat is purified)."[12]

---

[9]R. T. France, *The Gospel of Mark. New International Greek Testament Commentary* (Grand Rapids: Eerdmans,2002), 278.

[10]Bas M. F. van Iersel, *Mark: A Reader-Response Commentary* (England: Sheffield, 1998), 245.

[11]John Brunt, "Unclean or Unhealthful? An Adventist Perspective," *Spectrum* 11 (1981): 17-23.

[12]Robert W. Funk and Roy W. Hoover, *The Five Gospels: The Search for the Authentic Words of Jesus* (New York: Macmillan, 1993), 69.

Nineham on the other hand suggest that "It is doubtful that Jesus' first audience would imagine that he is encouraging them to eat swine, camel, or other meats forbidden by OT law."[13] There is no record of believers eating unclean meat in the New Testament.

Wahlen did a commendable work on Mark 7:19 by providing a historical element that food controversies continued until a few centuries after Jesus, which should not have existed at all if the early Christians understood that Jesus abolished food laws.[14]

Tim Hegg in his paper "Mark 7:19b—A Short Technical Note," notes some of the grammatical issues present in Mark 7:19 and makes a good case out of it. Hegg writes, "Does the fact that the participle καθαρίζων is nominative masculine mean that its only possible subject within the immediate context is Yeshua? Actually, there is another alternative. It is well known in

---

[13]D. E. Nineham, *The Gospel of St. Mark*. (Middlesex: Penguin Bks., 1963), 192.

[14]See Clinton Wahlen, *Jesus and the Impurity of the Spirits in the Synoptic Gospels* (Germany: Tubingen, 2004), 72-79; 142-44.

Greek grammar that the nominative singular participle may sometimes refer to something within the previous context or to something implied in the context not explicitly mentioned, even though it may not be in the same grammatical case."[15] Hegg concludes that, it is perfectly warranted to translate Mark 7:18-19 grammatically as "18 And He said to them, 'Are you so lacking in understanding also? Do you not understand that whatever goes into the man from outside cannot defile him, 19 because it does not go into his heart, but into his stomach, and goes out into the latrine, cleansing all foods (from the body)?"[16]

Summary

From the reviews above, it is clear that the statement "καθαρίζων πάντα τὰ βρώματα" in Mark 7:19 is widely taken to be a parenthetical comment issued by

---

[15]Tim Hegg, *"Mark 7:19b—A Short Technical Note,"* *Torah Resource, (May 2005), 2* accessed 29 September 2018, http://torahresource.com.

[16]Ibid., 5.

John Mark as narrator of this Gospel, to a predominantly non-Jewish, Roman audience, which might have asked questions about food and eating. This statement in Mark 7:19 is taking to be a Christological ruling that Jesus has declared all foods clean, thus abrogating the dietary laws in the Torah.

A minority view, takes all of v. 19 as being a part of the dialogue issued by Jesus, and that there has most likely been a translation error into English. This group understands that the phrase in Mark 7:19 is about cleansing food from the body and not declaring all foods clean. Thus Mark 7:19 has nothing to do with abrogating the dietary laws in the *Torah*.

CHAPTER 3

THE CONTEXT OF MARK 7:19

Mark 7:19 is within the broad context of Mark 7
which deals with purity. To understand the true meaning
of this verse calls for a study of the passage in its broad
context. This is necessary because in biblical
interpretation context determines meaning. This chapter
focuses on the historical context, literary context and
various backgrounds of Mark 7.

Historical Context

The books called *Gospels* deal with the life and
ministry of Jesus.[17] The gospels are Matthew, Mark,

____

[17]Robert Horton Gundry, *A Survey of the New Testament*
5th ed. (Grand Rapids, MI: Zondervan, 2012), 150.

Luke and John. This section of the research seeks to establish the authorship, date and place of composition of the Gospel according to Mark.

Authorship

Like the other gospels, there is still debate about the authorship of the Gospel according to Mark. The title, "According to Mark" (**καθα Μάρκον**) reveals the view of the early church. They never ascribed authorship of this Gospel to anyone other than Mark. The earliest testimony of Mark as the author is that of Papias, a bishop of Hierapolis in Phrygia of Asia Minor until about A.D. 130.[18]

---

[18]Carson, D. A. and and Douglas J. Moo *An introduction to the New Testament* 2nd ed (Grand Rapids, MI: Zondervan, 2005), 172. Carson asserts that "Christian writers of the second and third centuries confirm that Mark was the author of the second gospel and that he depended on Peter for his information: Justin Martyr, Dialogue with Trypho 106; Irenaeus, Adversus Haereses 3.1.2; Tertullian, Adversus Marcion 4:5; Clement of Alexandria, Hypotyposeis (according to Eusebius, H.E. 6.14.5–7); Origen, Commentary on Matthew (again according to Eusebius, H.E. 6.25.5); and, probably, the Muratorian Canon."

Gundry asserts that "the early church fathers Irenaeus, Clement of Alexandria, Origen, and Jerome also support authorship by Mark in association with Peter."[19] It is highly possible that John Mark who is mentioned in Acts (12:12, 25; 13:5, 13; 15:37) and in four New Testament epistles (Col. 4:10; Philem. 24; 2 Tim. 4:11; 1 Peter 5:13) is the one Papias and other early Christian writers had in mind.

Date of Writing

Lack of data to firmly establish the date of Mark's gospel has led to the proposition that the gospel was written either before or after the martyrdom of Peter (A. D. 64-67). After the assessment of facts dating Marks gospel to the 40s, the 50s, the 60s and the 70s,

---

[19]Robert Horton Gundry, *A survey of the New Testament* 5th ed. (Grand Rapids, MI: Zondervan, 2012), 150.

Carson and Douglas conclude that "We must be content with dating Mark sometime in the late 50s or the 60s."[20]

Audience and Provenance

There is no unanimous agreement about the place where Mark wrote this gospel. However, the anti-Marcionite prologue to Mark claims that it was written in the regions of Italy.[21] "Both Irenaeus (Adv. Haer. 3.1.2) and Clement of Alexandria (according to Eusebius, H.E. 6.14.6–7) suggest the same thing."[22] Other provenances are suggested by modern scholars but the Roman provenance seems the best option.

---

[20]Carson, D. A. and and Douglas J. Moo *An introduction to the New Testament* 2nd ed. (Grand Rapids, MI: Zondervan, 2005), 182.

[21] The Anti-Marcionite prologues to the Gospels are short prefixes to the gospels of Mark, Luke and John (see pages 101–2).

[22] Carson, D. A. and and Douglas J. Moo *An introduction to the New Testament* 2nd ed. (Grand Rapids, MI: Zondervan, 2005), 178

It is therefore highly probable that Mark wrote for a Roman audience. This is supported by his translations of Aramaic expressions in Mark 3:17, 5:41, 7:34, 14:36 and 15:34. He also explained Greek expressions using their Latin equivalents in Mark 12:42 and 15:16 and also uses a number of other Latin terms.[23]

Purpose of Writing

The gospel of Mark was written specifically to Gentile audience. At the time, crucifixion remained the punishment for criminals and slaves. Mark wrote to counteract the shame of the manner of Christ's death by stressing on his power to heal, raise the dead, cast out demons and other miracles he performed.

The work of Mark was designed as an apology to win Gentiles into the Christian faith despite the shame of the cross. Carson and Douglas asserts that Mark's

---

[23]Robert Horton Gundry, *A survey of the New Testament* 5th ed. (Grand Rapids, MI: Zondervan, 2012), 153.

purpose was to let his readers understand that Jesus is the
Son of God, but especially the suffering Son of God.
Thus helping them to understand who Jesus is and what
true discipleship involves.[24]

Literary Context

Literary context helps us to understand the
literary genre that the book of the Bible (the gospel of
Mark in this paper) exists in. It relates to the form a
passage takes and to the words, sentences, and
paragraphs that surround the passage in question.

Genre

Mark wrote as a preacher conveying God's good
news of salvation by emphasizing Jesus' saving ministry.
He also wrote as a theologian, arranging and interpreting

---

[24]Carson, D. A. and Douglas J. Moo *An introduction to the
New Testament* 2nd ed. (Grand Rapids, MI: Zondervan, 2005), 186.

the tradition to meet the needs of his hearers. The book of Mark is a gospel genre.

Language and style

The vocabulary of Mark's Gospel is limited. He uses 1,270 different words, of which 80 are peculiar to him among the NT writers.[25] Mark is fond of transliterating Latin words (at least ten of them) into Greek, and occasionally his Greek shows an underlying Latin construction or expression. A more important influence on Mark's language is Aramaic. Although Mark's facility with the Greek language is clearly inferior to that of Luke and other NT writers, he manages to achieve a remarkably forceful, fresh, and vigorous style. Another important feature of Mark's style is his vigorous interaction with his Readers.[26]

---

[25]Ibid., 611.

[26]William L. Lane, *The Gospel According to Mark.* NIC. (Grand Rapids: Eerdmans, 1974), 26.

Background Studies of Mark 7

Mark 7 begins with the coming together of the Pharisees and certain scribes which came from Jerusalem to Jesus. They saw some of Jesus' disciples eating with unwashed hands and questioned him: "Why do your disciples not live according to the tradition of the elders, but eat with hands defiled?"

The Ritual of hand washing

Mark explains in verses 3 and 4 that "the Pharisees, and all the Jews, do not eat unless they wash their hands, observing the tradition of the elders; and when they come from the market place, they do not eat unless they purify themselves." Josephus, the Jewish historian notes in *Antiquities of the Jews* 13.297 that, "the Pharisees have delivered to the people a great many observances by succession from their fathers, which are not written in the laws of Moses."[27] Handwashing, the main issue of Mark 7:1-23 is one of such observances.

---

[27]Flavius Josephus: *The Works of Josephus: Complete and Unabridged*, trans. William Whiston (Peabody, MA: Hendrickson, 1987), 355.

In the Mishnah is a summary of some of the traditions regarding handwashing: "He who pokes his hands into a house afflicted with *nega*—'his hands are in the first remove of uncleanness,' the words of R. Aqiba. And sages say, 'His hands are in the second remove of uncleanness.' Whoever imparts uncleanness to clothing, when in contact [with them], imparts uncleanness to the hands—'So that they are in the first remove of uncleanness, the words of R. Aqiba. And sages say, 'So that they are in the second remove of uncleanness.' Said they to R. Aqiba, 'When do we find that the hands are in the first remove of uncleanness under any circumstances whatsoever?' He said to them, 'And how is it possible for them to be in the first remove of uncleanness without his body's [being] made unclean, outside of the present case?' 'Food and utensils which have been made unclean by liquids impart uncleanness to the hands so that they are in the second remove of uncleanness,' the words of R. Joshua. And sages say, 'That which is made unclean by a Father of Uncleanness imparts uncleanness to the hands. [That which has been made unclean] by an Offspring of Uncleanness does not impart uncleanness to the hands.'...Said sages, 'The matter is clear. That which has been made unclean by a Father of Uncleanness imparts uncleanness to the hands. [That which has been made unclean] by an Offspring of Uncleanness does not impart uncleanness to the hands'" (m.*Yadayim* 3:1).[28]

Also, it is witnessed in the *Letter of Aristeas* that "Following the custom of all the Jews, they washed their hands in the sea in the course of their prayers to God."[29]

In the Torah it is found in Exodus 30:19 and 40:31 that the priests were commanded to wash their hands.

In the Talmud it is written: "*When he washes his hands, he says,* 'Blessed is he who has sanctified us by his commandments and commanded us concerning hand-washing'" (b. *Berachot* 60b).[30]

---

[28]Jacob Neusner, trans., *The Mishnah: A New Translation* (New Haven and London: Yale University Press, 1988), 1126.

[29]R. J. H. Shutt, "Letter of Aristeas," in James H. Charlesworth, ed., *The Old Testament Pseudepigrapha*, Vol 2 (New York: Doubleday, 1985), 33.

[30]*The Babylonian Talmud: A Translation and Commentary*. MS Windows XP. Peabody, MA: Hendrickson, 2005. CD-ROM.

Witherington III writes: "It was Pharisaic practice to wash diligently before eating. In order to understand the Pharisees, one must recognize that they attempted to apply the Levitical laws for the cleanliness of priests to everyone (see Exod. 30:19; 40:13). They in a sense believed in a real priesthood of all believers, and therefore all the Jews were called to priestly cleanliness."[31]

Though it was a common observance to practice handwashing, the Pharisees had an ulterior motive of casting doubt on Jesus' ministry by asking this question. Jesus knowing their motives rebuked them by calling them hypocrites. Having finished with that, Jesus called the people to him again, and said to them, "Hear me, all of you, and understand: there is nothing outside a man which by going into him can defile him; but the things which come out of a man are what defile him."

---

[31]Ben Witherington III, *The Gospel of Mark: A Socio-Rhetorical Commentary* (Grand Rapids: Eerdmans, 2001), 224.

Purity and Defilement

The Jews had many customs that dealt with defilement. Defilement is categorized into two: cultic and moral impurity. According to Jonathan Klawans, moral impurity is associated with sin more than the other.[32] Milgrom asserts that cultic impurity is "bodily impurity (defilement) which can be removed by ritual ablution" while moral impurity "is caused by inadvertent violation of prohibited commandments (Lev 4:2), and requires no purificatory rite."[33] Handwashing as it appears in the text perhaps might be classified under cultic impurity held in high esteem among the Pharisees and the scribes.

Jesus' statement in verse 15 takes away attention from cultic impurity to moral impurity. "What enters people from the outside (v. 15) refers to the food they

---

[32]See Jonathan Klawans, *Impurity and Sin in Ancient Judaism* (New York: Oxford University Press, 2000), 3-42.

[33]Jacob Milgrom, *Leviticus 1-16: A New Translation with Introduction and*
Commentary, AB, vol. 3 (Garden City, NY: Doubleday, 1991), 254; P. D. Miller, 151.

eat, and what comes out of people refers to their conduct; so the thesis proposed in these sayings is that human defilement is not caused by food but by evil actions. From this it follows that just as the stomach, along with what enters it, is opposed to the heart and to what comes out of it, so ritual impurity caused by unclean food is opposed to moral impurity, showing itself in wrong actions. Only the second form of impurity is recognized by Jesus."[34]

Unfortunately, the disciples did not understand the parable and so Christ had to explain it to them when he went to the house with them. "And he said to them, 'Then are you also without understanding? Do you not see that whatever goes into a man from outside cannot defile him, since it enters, not his heart but his stomach, and so passes on?' (Thus he declared all foods clean.)." Here is the confusion among scholars and the rest of the paper will focus on the Greek "καθαρίζων πάντα τὰ

---

[34]Bas M. F. van Iersel, *Mark: A Reader-Response Commentary* (England: Sheffield, 1998), 246.

βρώματα" that has been rendered in many modern translations as "Thus he declared all foods clean."

CHAPTER 4

EXEGESIS OF MARK 7:19

Many modern Christians have used Mark 7:19 to
substantiate the point that Jesus declared all foods clean
thus abrogating the dietary laws in the Torah. This
creates confusion because throughout the New
Testament, Jesus and the apostles are not found eating
anything unclean. How could he then issue such a
declaration? The problem is with how many bible
scholars have translated "καθαρίζων πάντα τὰ
βρώματα;" as "Thus he declared all foods clean"
(NASB, RSV, NRSV, ESV) in Mark 7:19.

Establishing the Text in Mark 7:19

The basic issue of this verse is the word
καθαρίζων. Three variations of this word appears in

manuscripts: 1. καθαρίζων 2. καθαρίζον and 3. καθαρίζεί. This has given rise to different translations of the text.

The Textus Receptus has καθαρίζον πάντα τὰ βρώματα. The word καθαρίζον is parsed as neuter singular nominative participle which modifies πᾶν τὸ ἔξωθεν εἰσπορευόμενον ("everything which goes in from without" in v. 18). However, there is evidence of καθαρίζον only after the ix century. This might have occurred due to the difficulty attached to καθαρίζων in the original manuscript.

The word καθαρίζων is parsed as masculine singular nominative participle. This reading "καθαρίζων πάντα τὰ βρώματα" is supported by older and more reliable manuscripts.[35] From a text critical standpoint on the obvious weight of textual evidence, Tim Hegg argues

---

[35]See the UBS[4] for lists of supporting data.

that, the original reading is καθαρίζων instead of καθαρίζον.[36]

In this case the closest antecedent masculine singular noun is ἀφεδρῶνα (toilet), which seems to create a grammatical problem since participles generally must agree in gender, number and case. Many modern scholars, following Origen and Chrysostom, regard καθαρίζων as connected with λέγει in verse 18 grammatically, and take it as the evangelist's comment.[37]

Therefore, the most preferred reading of Mark 7:19 is that found in UBS[4]: ὅτι οὐκ εἰσπορεύεται αὐτοῦ εἰς τὴν καρδίαν ἀλλ᾽ εἰς τὴν κοιλίαν, καὶ εἰς τὸν ἀφεδρῶνα ἐκπορεύεται, καθαρίζων πάντα τὰ βρώματα;

Translation of the Passage in Mark 7:19

Greek	English

---

[36]Tim Hegg, *"Mark 7:19b—A Short Technical Note," Torah Resource, (May 2005), 1* accessed 29 September 2018, http://torahresource.com.

[37] Bruce M. Metzger, *A Textual Commentary On The Greek New Testament* (London NY: United Bible Society, 1971), 95.

ὅτι	because
οὐκ	not
εἰσπορεύεται	it enters
αὐτοῦ	of him
εἰς	into
τὴν	the
καρδίαν	heart
ἀλλ'	but
εἰς	into
τὴν	the
κοιλίαν	belly
καὶ	and
εἰς	into
τὸν	the
ἀφεδρῶνα	latrine
ἐκπορεύεται,	it goes out,
καθαρίζων	cleansing/purging
πάντα	all

τὰ	the
βρώματα;	foods?

The text could be translated as "because it does not enter into the heart of him but into the belly and it goes out into the latrine, purging all foods?"[38] This is close to the rendering of the King James Version of the Bible: "Because it entereth not into his heart, but into the belly, and goeth out into the draught, purging all meats?" (Mark 7:19).

Grammatical/Syntactical Analysis: "καθαρίζων πάντα τὰ βρώματα;"

The Greek reading of Mark 7:19: ὅτι οὐκ εἰσπορεύεται αὐτοῦ εἰς τὴν καρδίαν ἀλλ᾽ εἰς τὴν κοιλίαν, καὶ εἰς τὸν ἀφεδρῶνα ἐκπορεύεται, καθαρίζων πάντα τὰ βρώματα; seems to have a grammatical problem. The closest antecedent masculine noun to καθαρίζων is

---

[38] Author's literal translation of Mark 7:19.

ἀφεδρῶνα (from ἀφεδρών). The grammatical problem is because participles must agree in gender, number and case with the noun to which they attach. The ἀφεδρῶνα is in the accusative case while καθαρίζων is in the nominative case.

It seems likely that some scribes had a difficulty understanding what stood as the subject of καθαρίζων since the obvious meaning seems to be that the elimination of the excrement is the subject. Trying to correct it, they employed the neuter gender participle, καθαρίζον.

It behoves us to look for the correct antecedent masculine noun which is the subject for καθαρίζων. Origen traces the subject to that of λέγει in verse18 which is Jesus.[39] William L. Lane, asserts that Origen's interpretation has won almost universal support.[40]

---

[39] Origen, *Commentary on Matthew,* Book 12, section 11.

[40]William L. Lane, *The Gospel According to Mark*, New International Commentary on the New Testament (NICNT) (Grand Rapids: Eerdmans, 1974), 253

Taking "Jesus" as the subject as proposed by Origen would render the translation "He (Jesus) is cleansing all the foods." Thus taking the entire context of the passage into consideration, it will be more correct to translate "καθαρίζων πάντα τὰ βρώματα" this way: "[He (Jesus)] is cleansing all foods." This is the reason for "Thus he declared all foods clean" as rendered in many modern English translations.

But is this correct? Does the fact that καθαρίζων is nominative masculine participle mean that its only possible subject within the immediate context is Jesus? Tim Hegg directs our attention to another alternative in Greek Grammar. Tim writes: "it is well known in Greek grammar that the nominative singular participle may sometimes refer to something within the previous context or to something implied in the context not explicitly mentioned even though it may not be in the same grammatical case."[41] He cites the following

---

[41]Tim Hegg, 2. See also F. Blass and A. Debrunner, *A Greek Grammar of the New Testament and Other Early Christian Literature* (Univ. of Chicago, 1961), 76; James Hope Moulton and Nigel Turner, A Grammar of New Testament Greek, 3 vols. (T&T

examples to buttress his argument: Luke 24:47, 2 Thessalonians 1:8 and James 3:8. In all these verses, there is a disagreement between a nominative masculine participle in case with its apparent antecedent.

For example, in Luke 24:47: "and that repentance and forgiveness of sins should be preached in his name to all nations, beginning from Jerusalem." (καὶ κηρυχθῆναι ἐπὶ τῷ ὀνόματι αὐτοῦ μετάνοιαν εἰς ἄφεσιν ἁμαρτιῶν εἰς πάντα τὰ ἔθνη. ἀρξάμενοι ἀπὸ Ἰερουσαλὴμ). Tim notes that "the participle in the clause 'beginning from Jerusalem' is nominative masculine plural, but there is no nominative masculine plural noun in the preceding context to act as its antecedent. It presumes an understood subject in the infinitival clause κηρυχθῆναι … μετάνοιαν, 'to preach…repentance,' something like αὐτοί κηρυξουσιν …μετάνοιαν … ἀρξάμενοι ἀπὸ Ἰερουσαλὴμ, 'they preach…repentance…beginning from Jerusalem.'"

Clark, 1963), 3.316; Maximilian Zerwick S. J., *Biblical Greek* (Pontificii Instituti Biblici, 1963), 5, 6.

Fortunately enough, the Greek Grammars cited by Tim reference Mark 7:19 as an example of a nominative masculine participle that does not agree in case with its apparent antecedent.

Those who take καθαρίζων πάντα τὰ βρώματα as Mark's comment do so on two grounds: 1. that καθαρίζων requires a masculine noun for its antecedent and 2. that Mark is known to interject his own explanatory comments. But this creates more difficulties when considering the general context of Mark 7.

However, if we apply the understanding gained from Greek grammar that καθαρίζων can have an antecedent with which it does not share grammatical concord, the difficulty of considering "καθαρίζων πάντα τὰ βρώματα" as Mark's comment is removed. Thus the antecedent of καθαρίζων could be either ἀφεδρῶνα or the excrement itself.

Word Study: "Καθαρίζων"

The word "καθαρίζων" is used only once in the New Testament (Mark 7:19).[42] The root word is καθαρίζω. Καθαρίζω is used in Matthew 23:25; Luke 11:39, as "to cleanse, render pure, or to purify." In Matthew 8:2, 3; 10:8, it is used as "to cleanse from leprosy." In Hebrews 9:22, 23; 1 John 1:7, it means "to cleanse from sin, purify by an expiatory offering, or make expiation for." In Acts 15:9; 2 Corinthians 7:1, it is used as "to cleanse from sin or free from the influence of error and sin." And in Acts 10:15; 11:9, it is used as "to pronounce ceremonially clean."[43]

In the BDAG, καθαρίζω could mean any of the following: *to make physically clean, make clean, cleanse; to heal a person of a disease that makes one ceremonially unclean, make clean, heal (esp. leprosy); to purify through ritual cleansing, make clean, declare*

---

[42] Mounce William D, *Analytical Lexicon to the Greek New Testament* (Grand Rapids: Zondervan, 1993), s.v. "καθαρίζων."

[43] William, s.v. "καθαρίζω."

clean. Bauer sees καθαρίζων as found in Mark 7:19 to mean "to make physically clean," "make clean" or "cleanse."[44] However, there is an assertion that, many scholars following the path of Origen prefer to take καθαρίζων as found in Mark 7:19 to mean "declare clean." These scholars regard "καθαρίζων πάντα τὰ βρώματα" as the evangelist's observation or a marginal note by a reader.[45]

In the Septuagint, καθαρίζω could mean any of the following: *to make clean, remove* dirt or impure substance *from:* of metal refining, (See Prov 25:4); *to render ritually or morally clean and acceptable (See* Ex 30:10, Lev 8:15, Deut 19:13, Num 31:23); *to perform the ritual of purgation (See* Lev 16:20); *to judge as morally pure (see* Ex 20:7; 34:7; Num 14:18); *to declare ritually clean (See* Lev 13:6); or *to make oneself clean ritually*

---

[44]Walter Bauer, *A Greek-English Lexicon of the New Testament and Other Early Christian Literature (BDAG),* 3d ed., ed. Frederick W. Danker (Chicago: University of Chicago Press, 2000), s.v. "καθαρίζω."

[45]Bauer, BAGD, s.v. "καθαρίζω"

and religiously by removing objects of paganism, (See Ge 35:2; Is 66:17).[46]

Since καθαρίζων has been used differently in both the NT and other early writings, what does it actually mean in Mark 7:19? Can καθαρίζων here mean "to purge"? Davidson asserts that "it is true that in the NT, it normally refers to cleansing in a religious sense, either through ceremonies or by a cleansing of conscience through forgiveness.[47] But it is no guarantee that Mark 7:19 does not use it in the sense of purging. We have already seen that in the LXX, it is used of physical cleansing (purging), though often figuratively (Ps 51:7; Ezek 38:30; Sir 38:30). This is of no less significance since the NT writers (and the Christian outside Palestine) generally used the Greek version of the OT.[48] Thus, καθαρίζων may actually mean 'to

---

[46]T. Muraoka, *A Greek-English Lexicon of the Septuagint* (Walpole, MA: Peeters, 2009), s.v. "καθαρίζω."

[47]Michael Morrison, "Are Some Meats Unclean?" 1995 [article on-line]; available from http://www.wcg.org/lit/law/unclean.htm; Internet; accessed 11 October 2018.

purge.'[49] If this is the case, it greatly contributes to
solving the issue involved in Mark 7."[50]

---

[48]Roger Nicole, "The New Testament Use of the Old
Testament," in *The Right
Doctrine from the Wrong Texts: Essays on the Use of the Old
Testament in the New*," ed.
G. K. Beale (Grand Rapids: Baker, 1994), 18, 19.

[49]Bauer, BAGD, s.v. "καθαρίζω." Mark 7:19 in the
Peshitta Version reads, "For it doth not enter into his heart, but into
his belly, and is thrown into the digestive process, which carries off
all that is eaten." This view, that καθαρίζω in Mark 7:19c is linked
to what immediately precedes it, is exemplified by Matthew Black,
An Aramaic Approach to the Gospels and Acts, 2d ed. [Oxford:
Oxford University Press, 1954], 217). Lenski, *Mark*, 297, concurs:
"The participial clause is beyond question a part of the explanation
of Jesus. He is explaining to His disciples how no food defiles a
man. The nominative case of the participle is not all important; in
the Greek the participle lends itself to constructions like the one we
have here. We read this nominative καθαρίζω just as if it were an
accusative, for it modifies the accusative ἀφεδρῶν." Others who
support this view include Henry Alford, *Alford's Greek Testament:
An Exegetical and Critical Commentary*, vol. 1, *Matthew-John*
(Grand Rapids: Baker, 1980), 360; John Albert Bengel, *New
Testament Word Studies*, vol. 1, *Matthew-Acts* (Grand Rapids:
Eerdmans, 2002), 338; Adam Clarke, *Commentary on the Bible*,
abridged by Ralph Earle (Grand Rapids: Baker, 1967), 842; H.
Ridderbos, 332, n. 35, says the "process of digestion is at the same
time the purification of the food" to which Moskala, 374, agrees.

[50]Davidson Razafiarivony, "The New Testament Attitude
Toward The Old Testament Distinction Between Clean And
Unclean Animals" (Doctor of Philosophy Dissertation, Adventist
International Institute of Advanced Studies, Philippines, 2006), 170,
171.

Considering the context of the passage, it is most likely that καθαρίζων means "*making clean*" or "*purging*" just as the King James Version of the Bible translates it and it is part of Jesus' statement and not the evangelist's comment or a marginal note as suggested by many modern English translators.

Theology and Message

From the discussions so far, it could be observed that the assertion of Mark 7:19 "declaring all foods clean," thus doing away with the dietary laws in the Torah suggested by many is problematic. This is because the assertion of Jesus in Mark 7:19 has absolutely nothing to do with the dietary laws in the Torah.

The context of Mark 7 as we have already seen was about failure on the part of the disciples of Jesus to observe ritual handwashing before eaten. The theology of Mark 7:19 is about what happens to food eaten with unwashed hands. The intention of Mark 7:19 as stated by Edwards is that "Food may enter the mouth, but it all ends up in the same place."[51]

Jesus actually spends time in Mark 7 to explain what actually defiles a man: "there is nothing outside a man which by going into him can defile him; but the things which come out of a man are what defile him." Jesus rebuked the Pharisees and the scribes against an over-reliance on external rituals and doing away with God's commandments. The prophets actually spoke against such attitude in the Old Testament and admonished the Israelites to obey God instead (see Isaiah 1:10-20 and Amos 5:21-27). Edwards' explanation is noteworthy: "Uncleanness and defilement are matters of intention and the heart, not the violation of cultic rituals and formalities."[52]

According to Guelich, "The community in no way understood Jesus' 'original' response in 7:15 to be

---

[51] James R. Edwards, *Pillar New Testament Commentary: The Gospel According to Mark* (Grand Rapids: Eerdmans, 2002), 212.

[52] Ibid., 212, 213.

in reference to the Levitical food laws. In fact, it was precisely the Pharisees' use of 'tradition' to contravene the Mosaic law that made them 'hypocrites.' So one could evidently still take seriously 7:15, buttressed by the argument in 7:6-13, in the narrow terms of 'defiled hands' and follow the Levitical food laws."[53]

The message of Mark 7 has nothing to do with the dietary laws in the Torah. Mark 7 actually conveys the message that defilement and uncleanness are matters of the heart. The parallel of Mark 7 in the gospel according to Matthew states that "Do you not see that whatever goes into the mouth passes into the stomach, and so passes on? But what comes out of the mouth proceeds from the heart, and this defiles a man. For out of the heart come evil thoughts, murder, adultery, fornication, theft, false witness, slander. These are what defile a man; but to eat with unwashed hands does not defile a man" (Matthew 15:17-20).

---

[53]Robert A. Guelich, *Word Biblical Commentary: Mark 1-8:26*, Vol. 34a (Dallas: Word Books, 1989), 376.

Interpretation of Mark 7:19

In many modern English translations, καθαρίζων
πάντα τὰ βρώματα; is rendered as "Thus he declared all
foods clean" in Mark 7:19. This is because in Mark 7:18
preceding, λέγει, "He says," a third person active
singular, agrees with καθαρίζων, a nominative (case
indicating subject) masculine present active participle.
Cranfield concludes that καθαρίζων πάντα τὰ
βρώματα; is a statement reliant upon λέγει. [54]

It is, of course, possible to view the
clause καθαρίζων πάντα τὰ βρώματα; in Mark 7:19, in
line with some agreement with λέγει in Mark 7:18, and
conclude that the statement did not intend to nullify the
dietary laws in the Torah, but instead issue a declaration
that the Biblically permitted foods can be eaten with
unwashed hands. Stern concludes in his *Jewish New
Testament Commentary* that "Yeshua did *not*, as many
suppose, abrogate the laws of *kashrut* and thus declare
ham *kosher!* Since the beginning of the chapter the

---

[54]C.E.B. Cranfield, *Cambridge Greek Testament
Commentary: The Gospel According to St. Mark* (Cambridge, UK:
Cambridge University Press, 1972), 241.

subject has been ritual purity as taught by the
Oral *Torah* in relation to *n'tilat-yadayim* (vv.2-4&N) and
not *kashrut* at all! There is not the slightest hint
anywhere that foods in this verse can be anything other
than what the Bible allows Jews to eat, in other
words, *kosher* foods."[55]

However, Tim Hegg in his paper "Mark 7:19b—
A Short Technical Note," notes some of the grammatical
issues present in Mark 7:19 and makes a good case out
of it. Hegg writes, "Does the fact that the participle
καθαρίζων is nominative masculine mean that its only
possible subject within the immediate context is Yeshua?
Actually, there is another alternative. It is well known in
Greek grammar that the nominative singular participle
may sometimes refer to something within the previous
context or to something implied in the context not

------

[55]David H. Stern, *Jewish New Testament
Commentary* (Clarksville, MD: Jewish New Testament Publications,
1995), 241.

explicitly mentioned, even though it may not be in the same grammatical case."[56]

Hegg concludes that, it is perfectly warranted to translate Mark 7:18-19 grammatically as "18 And He said to them, 'Are you so lacking in understanding also? Do you not understand that whatever goes into the man from outside cannot defile him, 19 because it does not go into his heart, but into his stomach, and goes out into the latrine, cleansing all foods (from the body)?"[57]

With the above translation of Mark 7:18, 19, the phrase "καθαρίζων πάντα τὰ βρώματα" explains that when food passes out from the stomach to the latrine, the process cleanses all foods from the body. It should never be understood from this phrase that Jesus declared all foods clean and thus abrogated the dietary laws in the Torah. Jesus never intended that man should eat

____

[56]Tim Hegg, *"Mark 7:19b—A Short Technical Note,"* *Torah Resource, (May 2005), 2,* accessed 29 September 2018, http://torahresource.com.

[57]Ibid., 5.

anything unclean. Neither did Mark make any such comment.

Applications of Mark 7:19

The message of Jesus in Mark 7 is very clear. Jesus in Mark 7 explains what actually defiles a man: the things which come out of a man are what defile him. We should be very careful with what comes out from the heart rather than an over-reliance on external rituals, for out of the heart come evil thoughts, murder, adultery, fornication, theft, false witness, slander. These are what defile a man; but to eat with unwashed hands does not defile a man.

Also, all should bear in mind that Mark 7:19 has absolutely nothing to do with the dietary laws in the Torah. No one should use this text in a sense that abrogates the dietary laws in the Torah that was given for our own benefit of good health. It could be that many Christians following the argument that Jesus declared all foods clean did that out of ignorance. The good news is that in times of ignorance God overlooked. He will forgive those who have not treated the body temple with carefulness by eating anything due to ignorance if they will desire to eat and drink to the glory of God from today.

CHAPTER 5

SUMMARY AND CONCLUSIONS

In this study, the much debated verse of the Bible has been thoroughly investigated. It seems clear to me that Origen did not understand the Greek grammar very well as has been explained by recent Greek grammarians. His explanation that "Jesus declared all foods clean" and so the dietary laws are not binding on modern Christian is a serious theological error that must be critically looked at and be avoided. As has been seen in this paper, Mark 7 was actually about defilement caused by eaten with unwashed hands. The passage has absolutely nothing to do with the dietary laws in the Torah.

Even though some scholars have suggested that it is possible to view the clause καθαρίζων πάντα τὰ βρώματα; in Mark 7:19, in line with some agreement with λέγει in Mark 7:18, and conclude that the statement did not intend to nullify the dietary laws in the Torah, but instead issue a declaration that the Biblically permitted foods can be eaten with unwashed hands, this conclusion is not faithful to the Greek text.

The weight of Greek grammatical evidence suggests that the nominative singular participle may sometimes refer to something within the previous context or to something implied in the context not explicitly mentioned, even though it may not be in the same grammatical case. Applying this understanding from Greek grammar that καθαρίζων can have an antecedent with which it does not share grammatical concord, the difficulty of considering "καθαρίζων πάντα τὰ βρώματα" as Mark's comment is removed. Thus the antecedent of καθαρίζων could be either ἀφεδρῶνα or the excrement itself. In this case, the best translation of Mark 7:18-19 agrees with the King James Version of the Bible: "[18] And he saith unto them, Are ye so without understanding also? Do ye not perceive, that whatsoever thing from without entereth into the man, *it* cannot defile him; [19] Because it entereth not into his heart, but into the belly, and goeth out into the draught, purging all meats?"

Thus as noted by Tim Hegg, whatever goes into the man from outside cannot defile him, because it does not go into his heart, but into his stomach, and goes out into the latrine, cleansing all foods from the body.[58]

In summary, the phrase "καθαρίζων πάντα τὰ βρώματα" in Mark 7:19 explains that when foods passes out from the stomach to the latrine, the process cleanses all foods from the body. It should never be understood from this phrase that Jesus declared all foods clean and thus abrogated the dietary laws in the Torah. Jesus never intended that man should eat anything unclean. Neither did Mark make any such comment.

____

[58]Ibid., 5.

BIBLIOGRAPHY

Aland, Black M., Martini M., Metzger M., and Wikgren A. *The Greek New Testament.* Stuttgart: United Bible Society, 2010.

B. Witherington III, *The Gospel of Mark: A Socio-Rhetorical Commentary.* Grand Rapids: Eerdmans, 2001.

Bauer, Walter. *A Greek-English Lexicon of the New Testament and Other Early Christian Literature. (BDAG),* 3d ed., ed. Frederick W. Danker. Chicago: University of Chicago Press, 2000.

Blass F. and A. Debrunner, *A Greek Grammar of the New Testament and Other Early Christian Literature.* Univ. of Chicago, 1961.

Brunt, John. "Unclean or Unhealthful? An Adventist
Perspective," *Spectrum* 11 (1981): 17-23.

C. Stettler, "Purity of Heart in Jesus' Teachings: Mark
7:14—23 Par. as an Expression of Jesus' Basileia
Ethics." *Journal of Theological* Studies 55
2467—502.

Carson, D. A. and and Douglas J. Moo *An introduction
to the New Testament* 2nd ed. Grand Rapids, MI:
Zondervan, 2005.

Chrysostom *Homilies on Matthew* 51.4 (NPNF, 10:318).

Clinton Wahlen, *Jesus and the Impurity of the Spirits in the
Synoptic Gospels.* Germany: Tubingen, 2004.

Cranfield, C. E. B. *Cambridge Greek Testament
Commentary: The Gospel According to St. Mark.*
Cambridge, UK: Cambridge University Press,
1972.

D. J. Rudolph, "Jesus and the Food Laws: A
Reassessment of Mark 7:19b." *Evangelical
Quarterly* 74:291-311.

Edwards, James R. *Pillar New Testament Commentary:
The Gospel According to Mark*. Grand Rapids:
Eerdmans, 2002.

Flavius Josephus: *The Works of Josephus: Complete and
Unabridged*, trans. William Whiston (Peabody,
MA: Hendrickson, 1987.

France, R. T. *The Gospel of Mark. New International
Greek Testament Commentary*. Grand Rapids:
Eerdmans, 2002.

Funk Robert W. and Hoover, Roy W. *The Five Gospels:
The Search for the Authentic Words of Jesus*.
New York: Macmillan, 1993.

Guelich, Robert A. *Word Biblical Commentary: Mark 1-
8:26*, Vol. 34a. Dallas: Word Books, 1989.

Gundry, Robert Horton. *A Survey of the New Testament*
5th ed. Grand Rapids, MI: Zondervan, 2012.

Iersel, Bas M. F. *Mark: A Reader-Response
Commentary.* England: Sheffield, 1998.

J. Marcus, Mark 1—8: A New Translation with
Introduction and Commentary. Anchor Bible 27.
New York: Doubleday, 2000.

Jacob Neusner, trans., *The Mishnah: A New
Translation* (New Haven and London: Yale
University Press, 1988.

Klawans, Jonathan. *Impurity and Sin in Ancient Judaism.*
New York: Oxford University Press, 2000.

Lane, William L. *The Gospel According to Mark.* NIC.
Grand Rapids: Eerdmans, 1974.

Maximilian, Zerwick S. J. *Biblical Greek.* Pontificii
Instituti Biblici, 1963.

Metzger, Bruce M. *A Textual Commentary On The Greek New Testament.* London NY: United Bible Society, 1971.

Michael Morrison, "Are Some Meats Unclean?" 1995. Accessed 30 September, 2018. http://www.wcg.org/lit/law/unclean.htm.

Milgrom, Jacob. *Leviticus 1-16: A New Translation with Introduction and Commentary*, AB, vol. 3. Garden City, NY: Doubleday, 1991.

Moulton, James Hope and Nigel Turner. *A Grammar of New Testament Greek, 3 vols.* T&T Clark, 1963.

Mounce, William D. *Analytical Lexicon to the Greek New Testament.* Grand Rapids: Zondervan, 1993.

Muraoka, T. *A Greek-English Lexicon of the Septuagint.* Walpole, MA: Peeters, 2009.

Nineham, D. E. *The Gospel of St. Mark*. Middlesex:
    Penguin Bks., 1963.

Origen, *Commentary on Matthew,* Book 12, section 11.

Razafiarivony, Davidson. "The New Testament Attitude
    Toward The Old Testament Distinction Between
    Clean And Unclean Animals." Doctor of
    Philosophy Dissertation, Adventist International
    Institute of Advanced Studies, Philippines, 2006.

Robert H. Stein, *Baker Exegetical Commentary on the
    New Testament,* ed. Robert W. Yarbrough and
    Robert H. Stein. Grand Rapids: Baker, 2008.

Roger Nicole, "The New Testament Use of the Old
    Testament," in *The Right Doctrine   from the
    Wrong Texts: Essays on the Use of the Old
    Testament in the New,*" ed. G. K. Beale.
    Grand Rapids: Baker, 1994.

Shutt, R. J. H. "Letter of Aristeas," in James H.
Charlesworth, ed., *The Old Testament
Pseudepigrapha*, Vol 2. New York: Doubleday,
1985.

Stern, David H. *Jewish New Testament Commentary*.
Clarksville, MD: Jewish New Testament
Publications, 1995.

Taylor, V. *The Gospel according to St. Mark: The Greek
Text with Introduction, Notes, and Indexes*.
London: MacMillan, 1952.

*The Babylonian Talmud: A Translation and
Commentary*. MS Windows XP. Peabody, MA:
Hendrickson, 2005. CD-ROM.

Tim Hegg, *"Mark 7:19b—A Short Technical Note," Torah
Resource, (May 2005)*. Accessed 29 September 2018.
http://torahresource.com.

Witherington III, Ben. *The Gospel of Mark: A Socio-Rhetorical Commentary.* Grand Rapids: Eerdmans, 2001.

www.ingramcontent.com/pod-product-compliance
Lightning Source LLC
Chambersburg PA
CBHW071236240726
48654CB00009B/1082